To the reader

Thank you for purchasing this book, life is made up of two unique events, Success or Failure.

Hidden in these pages is the secret to transform failure and adversity into long-awaited success. A book that will touch your soul.

It will make you discover the power that exists within you, so that you can make your dreams a reality.

Omar Hejeile Ch.

AUTHOR
Omar Hejeile Ch.

Editorial Wicca rescues the immeasurable power of the self and nature; a power everyone possesses, feels, and perceives, but few know. We share by means of texts and radio programs, without imposing a truth or a concept, so each one who feels the calling from within, who discovers the magic of dreams, and wishes to obtain the knowledge, thus, the transformation of their life can reach the center of

happiness.
The old religion has been reborn…
and it is in your hands.

WICCA
SCHOOL OF MAGIC

The old religion based on the magical knowledge of ancient cultures lost in time, escaped from the world of the hyperboreans, the harmony between man and nature are reborn like the phoenix.

Wicca, a term that comes from Wise, Wizard, means "The task of the wise", "The artisans of wisdom". During millennia of persecution, the ancient documents of the old religion remained hidden awaiting for the proper moment to be reborn; now, Wicca, recovers several of the old knowledge about the influence of the moon, the sun, the great Sabbats, the secret power of enchantments and spells, the art of incantations, the infinite magical world of plants, and the secret of the stars.

More information in:

www.ofiuco.com

www.radiokronos.com

www.wiccausa.com

Author: Omar Hejeile Ch.

Title: How To Avoid Failure And Have Success In 21 Days
ISBN:979-836-8160-85-6

Imprint: WICCA S.A.S (978-958-8391)
ENCYCLOPEDIA: "Universe of Magic".
Design and Layout: Mario Sánchez C.

www.ofiuco.com

HOW TO EVOID FAILURE AND HAVE SUCCES IN 21 DAYS

21 DAYS, SUCCESS OR FAILURE

During the winter, when the nights are long and heavy, the temple gets covered by the great power.

In the twilight, the clanging of the link in the gigantic portico is heard.

Cloaked, hidden within the hood, a young man waited.

The snow decorated the entrance falling in playful flakes.

Knock… Knock… Knock… A moment of silence, then the creak of the great doors opening; it sounded like a lament. .

- Good evening, good man, what brings you to the temple.

- Good evening «he sighed» I have come from far away, looking for a little peace, some wisdom in the face of my sorrow and pain… Would you give this pilgrim a place to stay?

- You seem to have lost your way, come, perhaps you will find the answers that stir your soul, altering your senses.

They wandered down the long corridor, the flickering torches gave a spectral touch, the shadows of the fluttering bats became ghostly figures. At the end of the corridor, in a small alcove, just a mat was all the decoration, a thick blanket for the cold, some water and a piece of bread.

- For now, you will spend the night here, it is warm, rest and tomorrow with the master, maybe you will find what you came for.

When the soul is distressed, reality is transformed, changing the meaning of thoughts, the mind is submerged in fantasy worlds of pain, despair, abandonment, denial becomes present, clouding reason.

The night was passing through the hours, in the distance, the rhythmic echo of the monks walking or perhaps the passing of the specters that do not rest.

The new day woke up gray, cloudy and rainy.

Kadaisha; sheathed in his robe, walked slowly, it seemed that he was floating, his great size, his strange feet and hands, as well as his only eye, produced more than fear, terror.

No one knows how or when the temple was built, no one knows where the master came from, there is no history, no memories, nothing, only mystery.

He is a cyclops from the confines of Shamballa.

A monk interrupted him:

- Master, this man came looking for help, he wants to discover the secrets of suffering, he wants to talk to you.

- What can I do for you?
With respectful permission, he said.

- Sir, the doors of my destiny have closed. Today, my existence has been covered with pain, sorrow and misfortune.

- Hopelessness has taken over my longings, now it is like this day, there is no light on my path, sadness accompanies me and this feeling of anguish does not leave me in peace.

- Do you really have and feel that?

- Yes master, this is my last halo of life, I see no way out, nor do I find peace in the face of adversity.

- Do you consider yourself finished, that there is nothing more for you in this world? Nothing more!? But you haven't realized, you arrived here, on a winter night, so even in your despair, there is still light.

- No, there isn't, my life has been a failure, I tried a thousand things, love, work, study, I struggled every day, in the end, it ended badly.

- So, your life has been a failure or at least, that's what you consider. Come with me!

They walked through the endless labyrinths, some smoking torches had extinguished their light, in the background the gate leading to the bridge of stakes, a merciless place.

THE MOAT OF STAKES

A bridge of wisdom

- *Walk across that narrow bridge, it is here that success or failure is found, life or death lies, it is here that you will face your fears, if you want to die, you will die, if you want to live, you will live.*

The man looked at the terrified monk, in front of him, a suspension bridge made of old timbers, without railings, suspended in the air.

Below, a few meters away, a moat of sharp, long stakes.

There were skulls, impaled skeletons, stakes covered with the remains of skeletal habits, stained with blood.

The man was petrified.

- *No, I can't pass that way, if I fall I will suffer a terrible death.*

- *You said that your light had been extinguished, that this is your last option. You are afraid to die, but do not wish to live?*

This is the bridge between life and death, or rather, if you prefer, between success and failure.

Even so, before you want to try something different, look back...

The door had disappeared, only centimeters separated them from an abyss carpeted by clouds, the bottom was not visible.

Kadaisha and the apprentice contemplated the bridge, twenty-one steps of aged wood, supported by fragile ropes.

Each plank holds a series of ancient inscriptions, a non-human language, sigils or stamps of profound wisdom.

- Cross it!

The man contemplated the depth of the moat, looked at the unstable bridge, the garden of stakes, without any support, shook his head as a gesture of denial.

- If I do; I will die.

- That's right, you don't start an enterprise without first being prepared to do it, listen well. A bridge is nothing more than the union between two shores, it is the link that unites the present with the future, a dream with reality.

In the actions of life, the illusions that are born, in the love that is professed, are united with invisible bridges. Likewise, those footbridges hang over daggers that will destroy you.

If you venture into daring actions, without preparing yourself, you will die! Undoubtedly, you will reach the other shore, but you must prepare yourself.

You will have to forget what you have learned, empty the glass of your conscience, you have it full of fears, anxieties, useless memories that hurt you, your frustration is not because of the apparent failure of your life, it is because you have never concluded; what you have started, have been failed attempts.

Life is a continuous learning process, the soul is trapped in deep pain, where sorrows accumulate.

The loneliness, the despair, the quick resignation, expecting too much of the unrealized becomes failure. Somehow, improvisations end up destroying great visions.

They take their toll on the spirit, they accumulate, preventing us from thinking, in this dramatic confinement, the only thing left to do is to escape and give up.

But, as the eternal echo repeats itself, one ends up convinced that nothing will be achieved.

It is inner fear, doubt and uncertainty that paralyzes the will, there is no movement of the soul, to progress. Denial, impossibility, wrong justifications are the reason for not facing adversity, accepting defeat.

THE FIRST STEPS

A path of power

The snow covered the slabs of the monastery in white, while some monks, deep in meditation, emptied other cups.

A little farther from the stairs, the valley of power, a plain that ends near the cliff, placed in a spiral form, several bridges, first on the grass, followed by others higher and higher, the last one; supported on unstable ropes, it borders the abyss.

- You will not do anything you do not know how to do, in order to achieve it; you must learn, train, act, overcome your fears, break the wall of your fears.

Now you will start, for the simple, this is the first railway, as you appreciate it is covered with tar, if you walk on it you will slip, so what is the first thing you should do?

- Clean it, dry it, remove the tar.

- Good, now get started! I suggest you do it slowly, so you won't start over.

The apprentice took the sponge, the bucket, the sand, slowly began the work, the black mixture covered his hands, the cold made the work more difficult.

Again and again, sand, tow, scrubbing and scrubbing, cleaning each part, suddenly... When you removed the layer that covered it, a strange symbol appeared.

- Now, clean that part carefully, you will see the first step shining, when you see the symbol, bring two buckets with water.

After endless hours, the sigil appeared refulgent, then he fulfilled the request.

✱ The First Arcanum
Surrender
Cizhi

- Master; What does this symbol mean

- It is the first lesson to discover the inner power, a book written in the wind that you must now read, it means; Surrender!

- Surrender? I have nothing to give up, there is nothing in my life, what would I even give up.

- You'll find out.

For now, go rest, tomorrow at dawn here we will meet again.

✴ Day One

A cold dawn, sore hands, there was the apprentice and his master, beginning the story of inner transformation to overcome adversity.

- Control the cold with your mind, make it part of you, it will be your trainer today.

- What should I do, Master.

- Remain calm... you are going to clean the snow off the plank, then, you will stand on it, take the buckets with this stick, put it on your shoulders and hold it until I come back.

But, you will not be able to let go, no matter what happens, even if it hurts, while you do so, you will review your whole life, your mistakes, you will let go of your pain, your unhappiness, you will let go of your unhappiness, for each one of them, you will overcome your emotion, holding the buckets.

When you feel desperate to quit, you will stand on one foot and find balance, then on the other, until you overcome and let go of your suffering.

If you consider that you will not succeed and you want to give up, the exit of the temple is on the side of those palm trees, you will never return.

Test yourself, you can do it!

I suggest you do it calmly, convince your mind that there is no cold, control your body, the buckets are not heavy, you and they are one.

- I will try, master.

- No, don't try, do it!

The monk began to perform the task, the water in the buckets had frozen, a layer of ice floated on the water. Standing with his arms at his sides, he held the weight, but, it was not as difficult as the war raging in the mind.

To test the will is a sacred art of concentration, to destroy the walls of the "I cannot", "impossible", "I am not capable", "it is difficult", "I will not succeed", "it is not easy." It requires inner power.

Time passed, fatigue accumulated, restlessness, despair, a struggle between giving up or winning. At the beginning, the mind gets lost in absurd thoughts, accustomed to not fighting or demanding itself, it tries to sneak away.

But, it is there, where the inner power takes over, the stillness is coming, contemplating the other monks in meditation does the same, relaxing the mind.

After endless hours, in deep calm, perched like the stork with outstretched arms, the mind of the apprentice was in stillness and repose, regardless of the cold, the weight or the fatigue.

He waited for the master, he had to remain there, the master would return, to free him from the test.

Time passed, despair began, the monologues flowed, What am I doing here? What am I going to get out of this? Should I leave? Why doesn't he come? Should I give up? No, I'd better try until he comes back, the feelings pile up, the pain is unbearable, tears flow like a balm in the face of impotence.

Fear increases, the anguish, the aching arms tremble. One suffers, but, deep down, the warrior rises, that voice that is rarely heard, that says "Go on!
A little more, push yourself, do it!

Darkness came and with it calmness, a full day of an inner battle, an apprentice holding two buckets of water.

Still, within his being, an incredible battle raged.

Near dawn, Kadaisha returned.

- You made it, I knew you would, carefully release the buckets, move your arms slowly. When you recover, take the resin, cover the arcane again, go to sleep.

- Master...
«With a gesture he stopped him»

- Now, say nothing, be silent, finish and sleep, later, after you rest; here I wait for you.

✳ Day Two
Second Arcanum
Harmony
Hexié

Just like the day before, they found themselves in front of the second sleeper, nothing covered it, but, it was supported on the tip of a small pyramid.

- The meaning of this sigil is harmony, after yesterday when your mind went into conflict, you are going to evaluate the MEANING of your life.

You will have to multitask, keep your balance on the board, evaluate within yourself the goodness of light and darkness.

You are going to look for what you have learned from what you have lived, try to understand what is good from bad and bad from good.

In your feelings, you are going to look inside yourself with all clarity, if you were looking for love or if you gave love.

In your thoughts, you are going to look at both ends, «while avoiding falling» when you are ready, you will take this cup with water, you will hold it in your hands, one at a time, if you get tired, change hands. It's up to you if the water spills.

Still avoid falling off the board.

- Master... «Again, he stopped him»

- I will tell you when we will talk, the answers are within you.

The apprentice started another task, he thought, how to climb up, to keep his balance holding the cup with water.

As we enter the mysterious world of wisdom, inner harmony is one of the most complex arts, inner harmony is one of the most complex arts, knowing the variation that exists in the duality of something

Two extremes and a center, a rhythm that rocks without stopping, traveling from one to the other.

In the temple, the sense of freedom is translated into two aspects; good or bad, but knowing the meaning in each one, is one of the mysteries of balance.

In the end, there is nothing good or bad, they are points of view, to win is good, to lose is bad, however, to lose is to learn, to discover, to err, to make mistakes or to succeed.

For this, one must see, search, analyze and understand where the other extreme is, to build on the destruction, to find the triumph hidden in the defeat.

The apprentice tried to climb, one foot, another foot... balancing, nothing. When something is unknown, it is necessary to fall or fail, but it is where failure becomes learning.

At the end of a few hours, he held on, juggling back and forth, eventually he overcame the cadence, slowly, his mind and energy harmonized, then stillness, balance, the cup.

In that stillness he closed his eyes and time passed. After midnight, the master returned.

- *You made it, come down from there, tell me, what is in your mind now.*

- Master, yesterday and today, these two boards have shown me that I was caught in a churning sea of emotions, a constant turbulence of thoughts.

I was blind to the world, only contemplating my problems, the past, the destructive events in my life.

Now, in spite of the physical fatigue, I feel that I have clarity, within my being there is serenity.

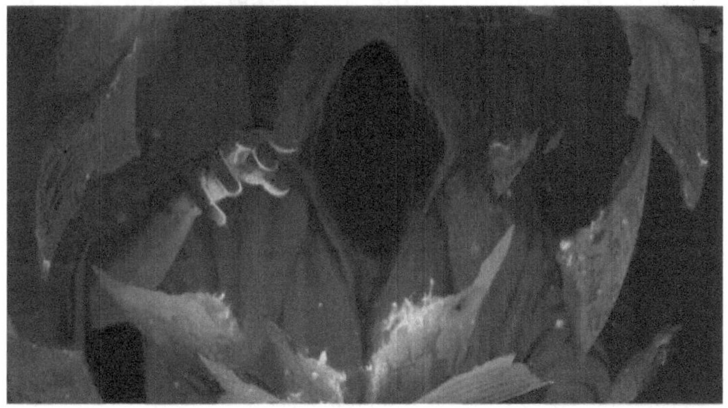

When life puts you to the test, but your soul is tied with the moments you consider adverse, is when you fall into the abyss of desolation.

»Feelings are altered, clouding reason, you get trapped inside you, you create a prison where you turn your mind into a prisoner who will never get out.

»Thus, again and again, you try to open that cell, but, you always fail, you consider then that you have failed, you blind yourself, you defeat yourself, you accept to be the prisoner of your acts.

»You crash against the bars of your thoughts, without finding a reason, you suppose, wrongly, that the world is against you.

»You go from one extreme to another without control, your fears lead you to accept defeat, without even having fought.

»Your soul enters the worst of conflicts, you have created the dungeon of failure in your mind, you have entered it and, although it has no lock, you locked yourself in.

» You lost the balance between your interior and your exterior, you go from one side to the other and the worst is that you accept it.

» Just like the plank, yesterday you had to overcome your pain, today you learned to control yourself, at the beginning you staggered, you made it! And the cup didn't spill over.

»Put on this blindfold, cover your eyes and climb the plank, but; you'll stand on one foot.

- One foot?

- Yes, you have in your mind, the power, Do it!

There, like an immovable statue, the apprentice, in a perfect equilibrium, stood until dawn.

When inner balance is found, harmony is discovered, one lives in the beehive of existence, the ups and downs of each day, constant sequences in perpetual rhythm, ebb and flow.

In the temple, duality shows that the extremes are reconciled in a gentle swaying.

✳ Day Three
Third Arcanum
Tai

- Look well, this stamp symbolizes the most fervent desire that exists in the soul, Peace, that feeling of deep serenity, where the conflict has ended.

» But, peace, entails in its essence, chaos, war, hostility, confrontation, inequality. Of the states of the soul, the most dangerous is peace.

» Fragile as a feather in the wind, temporary and ephemeral, there is no lasting peace, because even peace itself is conflict.

»It precedes and precedes storms, inner peace does not exist, you swing like a pendulum between two struggles, the one you leave behind and the one that will undoubtedly come.

» There is no peace that lasts more than an instant, it is broken by the breath of a breeze, destroyed by a thought, drowned by fear.

» It comes, after chaos, it appears out of nowhere, it is the ash left over from the destructive fire and from it, hopes spring.

» To keep the peace, is a difficult mission, but, you will be in harmony, if you know the signs of war.

E The apprentice began another experience, the plank, held in the air on two ropes, moved in the wind. Held in the air on two ropes, it moved with the wind, the snow on it made it slippery.

Placed in such a way that it slid on the ropes, a long descent, the height increased until it reached the end on a platform.

The sum of the previous two days, calm, serenity, mental and physical strength and balance, combined in time.

Confident he climbed on the board, the master told him:

- *Feel, not with your skin, but with your mind, feel in your being the soft signals that tell you where the balance is lost, compensate before the chaos, the slower, concentrated you do it, if you perceive the vibrations you will get far.*

»Allow your energy to go forward, you will feel the wind, the inclination, you will learn to fly, overcome your fear.

He started the descent, one knee to the side, balancing the swing, three or four meters, he destabilized and... rolled down.

A strong blow, cushioned by the snow, no one does something they don't know, no one tries to venture into undertakings without assessing the risks, but, falls are necessary in learning, even if they are considered a failure.

- Why do you think you failed?

- Master, I felt fear, I got out of control, I could not keep my balance, I went from side to side, until I fell.

- It wasn't your eyes or your body, it was your mind that altered them. Try something, you must trust your inner strength, put on this blindfold.

- With your eyes closed?

- No, blindfolded, so you can see with your senses, eyesight deceives, but if you feel without seeing, you will see the invisible, you will know before what is going to happen, do it!

Frightened, he climbed onto the sleeper, blindfolded himself, looked for balance, crouched down, arranged his feet and legs, hands at his sides, as if on skis.

He swayed, sharpened his senses, the center of gravity to be in balance, began... the descent.

The wind blew, the ropes vibrated changing the movement, at the beginning he sought to compensate slowly, then he picked up speed, he harmonized, a smooth and perfect descent. When he arrived he took off his blindfold, «jumping with joy» happy to have succeeded.

- *Learn to handle sadness and happiness in the same way, keep your emotions in balance.*

- *But master, for me it is an achievement.*

- *Even so, small unbridled joys also destabilize you by delaying your goal, it is the first sign of failure, now do it without the blindfold.*

Once, again, the emotions got in the way, he was upset, two, three meters, another fall, another attempt, four meters, another fall, he needed a day, to achieve what he did blindfolded in a minute; night came, the master was gone, but the apprentice was still practicing.

✻ Fourth, Fifth, Sixth and Seventh Arcane Day Shan The Mountain

After an agitated night, one more test to understand success or failure, the end or the beginning, to quit or to continue.

Life is a huge mountain, with ascents and descents, some easy, some steep, some steep, no two alike.

However, it always hides the fall into the abyss, which is, in itself, the security of the beginning, the mountain, is transformed into two extremes, life or death, success or failure.

You start from the safety of the ground, the higher you ascend, the deeper the abyss into which you fall, if you slip.

Likewise, the higher your undertaking, the greater the loss; if you lose your way.

The lessons hidden in the monastery, the apprentice was ready and Kadaisha appeared like a shadow in the mist.

- How is your soul today?

- Master, is happiness bad?

- There is nothing bad or good, happiness, like peace, lasts only a fleeting instant which, likewise, antecedes or precedes sadness.

»Peace, success, failure, pain, joy, passions are changeable, depending on the stimulus that alters them, they go from one polarity to another, the ideal state of the soul is to learn to be in balance.

»Al avanzar hacia una emoción, das el doble de espacio a la contraria, si subes dos metros, en tu caída, serán cuatro, aunque no puedas caer más allá de dos. Ya lo comprenderás.

»When you advance towards an emotion, you give double the space to the opposite one, if you go up two meters, in your fall, it will be four, although you cannot fall further than two. You will understand.

»Now, you will know the ebb and flow of existence, the changes, the unexpected, you must remember that, there is no such thing as stability.

»In nature, in the mind, in the cosmos, nothing is stable, a perpetual mutation governs the continuity of time and even time, has no stability.

- Master, if there is nothing stable, how do you control that balance? How do you know when change occurs?

- You've done it, in the previous days, it's not something that you reason or explain, it's an inner feeling, a faint change that ends up altering your spirit.

There, suspended in the air, a floating bridge with eight steps, four ascending, four descending, placed on two ropes, resembling the arms of a pedestal.

Separated by a space, placed on two movable ropes, thus; by moving a sleeper moves forward or backward, changes position, goes up on one side or the other.

At the end of the bridge, two monks cover their faces, each holding one of the ropes.

It will not be easy to walk eight steps, but, in the temple, it is about knowing the abrupt changes of life, always waiting for the unexpected.

He was scared, nervous, there is no protection rope, there is no mattress to receive him, there is nothing, it will depend on him.

He began to climb, it was noticeable how his mind calmed down and his senses expanded, more than seeing, he felt the changes in his feet.

But, after only three movements, he lost his balance and fell, he remained motionless on the snow.

The master was watching him with his only eye…

- *Do you consider this a failure?*

- *Yes, Master, I failed, I don't know what happened, I fell without control, I tried to be prepared, but the sudden movement surprised me.*

- *Life is that, the unexpected, even though you knew what could happen, it happened, there is a strange feeling in the soul, confidence, you assume that you are already qualified for something, when you are just starting to do it.*

»*That false security and the rush to achieve quick goals lead you to lose concentration, your mind is distracted, you do not evaluate, you do not feel, you trust that you will be able to, but you end up wrong.*

»Now, you feel defeated, you're shipwrecked looking for a Why? You don't know the reason for your frustration, the two options appear, you try until you make it or you quit.

»You'll need some time to start getting on the first, some more time on the second, and some time to get past it or maybe you never will.

»Only the seeming repetitive failure, leads you to the longed-for success.

»The more times you fall, you double your learning, so you must understand that failure does not exist.

»Success is achieved with small and constant failures. Just like life, whatever you do, you must learn from your mistakes.

»At nightfall, on the terrace, you will learn another lesson...

The day went by, he tried many times, he could not get past the first step.

You could feel the frustration, the anxiety, the helplessness. In the distance, the monks were training, some of them trying to walk on water.

Others, concentrated in strange positions, hugging a trunk with their legs, while hanging upside down.

In the temple, as in life, one must train the body and mind, physical inactivity leads to mental laziness. Start from nothing, advance, practice, try again and again.

By doing so; you create discipline, self-love, and by training, you increase your willpower to achieve your goals. On the contrary, being immobile damages the body and nullifies the spirit.

The short winter day faded, night came, on the terrace, near the abyss, the bonfire was lit, the flame of wisdom, another lesson of Kadaisha, an experience for the soul.

The monks gather, trapped in their hoods, listening to the stories of Kadaisha, legends full of wisdom.

When the master narrates, each one imagines that he is the actor of the story, applies it to his life, meditates on it, and finds the answers.

At the end of the corridor, he appeared sheathed in the habit, walking without eagerness, the master descends from the Cyclops, no one knows of his past.

He settled near the railing, the clouds served as a backdrop, shining with the lights of the lamps. The nuns and monks were ready to listen to the voice of the master:

Kadaisha spoke

«Is not the experience worth more than the treasure? The one is lost, the other is perpetuated in eternity.

The soul struggles between possessing and being, nothing is worth the knowledge of those who have lived to learn.

Mastery is the art of knowing how to fail, perhaps better; to find the path that leads to success and therefore to fulfillment, the fullness has no end, failure is where you learn, always... A little more.

Long ago... in the distant land, beyond the sea, where the beaches kiss the sands of the vast desert. A nomad of time... As a camel driver, began to work.

He knew nothing of the dunes, the camels, the oasis, and he knew less to see in the stars the paths that mark the places.

Nothing... an apprentice of life, however, he had the need to do something for his empty existence, he thought it was easy in what he would go to work.

Who explains to a fool what he does not want to know? He must feel and learn, alone... He will achieve it by facing adversity.

The camel driver set out on his journey, he supposed that the sweltering heat would be his shelter, that like the camels, he would not be thirsty.

Without any preparation, he ventured through the labyrinths of the desert, he carried a load and ten camels, an old map that showed him where... he should rest.

The hot sun, the sand, the wind, he didn't even know how to use the shemagh, (Bedouin Scarf) on the contrary, he took off his clothes, something he shouldn't do.

The day traveled nowhere, at nightfall he understood, he was lost.

The dromedaries, calmly, laid down to ruminate one next to the other.

Night fell... his first night in the desert, he tried in vain a thousand times to set up the tent, but he could not even light the fire.

He cursed in despair that he had ventured out, he wept, after a day of intense heat, the night chilled him to freezing.

Not knowing where he was, there was no path to return, no signposts, no way forward.

One long night, without water, he thought he would soon die, he looked at the camelids, the load, the desert, he looked at his feet in the sand, he entered the desolation, and tired, so he fell asleep.

He woke up... for a few moments, the man supposed it was a nightmare, the reality is there, alone in the desert, depending on his strength to save his life.

He searched through the saddlebags for something to eat, but, there was nothing, the animals of the night consumed his few viands.

The sun rose, the wind shook the dunes changing the landscape, the nomads say... that the desert has life, it transforms, it changes, it goes crazy.

It didn't take long... hunger, heat, thirst, came together, he began to have visions, mirages appeared, water sources, rivers, food, he got up hoping to be close... but... the hallucination faded away.

Another day, not knowing what to do, the caravan lying down, the camels calmly waiting for the order to move forward.

A difficult situation, in the soul, in the work, in the daily life, there are deserts that, although they hide happiness, you must first get to know them.

Several days passed, the man was depressed, he had no more tears, he saw his life pass several times, the memories... He felt sorry for the animals, he knew he was going to die.

When adversity comes, denial makes its appearance, the apparent failure induces the mind to question why it did what it did.

But somehow, there is always a force within that drives one to continue, that strange being that sleeps within, above the pain! It wakes up and pushes.

The camels became restless, they had no guide, yet they knew the way to the oasis. As if they were one, in time, they got up and began the journey.

He started following the camels, as he continued in his lamentations. Self-pity is the worst enemy of advancement.

Suddenly...! He changed his thinking, «sure, they know where to go.»

With the serenity that comes after the storm, the options awaken, letting himself be guided by the dromedaries, they arrived at the oasis, the fresh water, the dates, the vegetation.

The temporary end of failure, an oasis for the soul, always; there are such oases in life.

The intense heat, the man undressed, diving several times, but the water was hot, the change that occurs between despair and calm is a fragile line, where everything seems to be wrong.

Without knowing what to do, in the strange laws of the universe, a being who is ready to teach appears.

You can call it whatever you want, an angel, a teacher, a demon, goblins, genies…they do not always have a human form.

A book, a newspaper, a song, a single phrase, a comment, even a symbol, can reveal a new path.

That›s something! That the great majority disregards, ignores or rejects, the struggle of the ego, which only in desperation, cries out for help.

His musings were broken, as he observed a column of smoke, he thought, it›s another hallucination, however... he walked the short distance.

Wrapped in a tunic, covering his head with the turban, while lighting the bonfire, it was «the desert dweller». An old old man, weather-beaten by the sands, looked at him with some astonishment.....

- *You›re not from this place. What are you doing here, so far from home?*

- I don›t know, I took a job as a camel driver and I was supposed to take this caravan, but I got lost. The camels brought me.

- And, you, who are you?

- I am a nomad, this is my home, I travel guiding pilgrims who, like you, end up lost.

- Don›t you get lost? How do you guide yourself?

While I was putting some meat on the coals....

- The desert has many paths, shortcuts, avenues, signs, markings, signs that tell you where you are, where to go, just like the big city.

- Are you kidding me, there is no such thing?

- Wait for the night, you'll see them. Let me see what you have in your bags.

"Looking through the luggage" he was placing, in an orderly fashion, the tent, the clothes, a knife, a flint and a couple of empty canteens.

»"You have what you need, but it's no use having it if you don't know how to use it.

- I assumed that I could do it... but...

He was interrupted...

- But nothing! The same apology, people venture into a world they don't know, they underestimate reality, they don't think. However, you will learn if you want to. I have all the time in the world.

- Will you teach me?

- No, you are the one who learns from the path, it exists, it is your freedom, if you discover what it hides, I will only show it to you, you walk it.

»Now, enjoy your dinner...

- What is it?

- Desert rat, it tastes good and will give you strength. If you don't want it, starve. Hunger will make you eat. If you want to live in the desert, you must accept, what it gives you.

So, the man... began to assume that he failed.

Next to the dweller, he found the most fantastic lesson in life, "The more you make mistakes, fail and without defeating yourself, try again, you will be a master."

He discovered the way to find food, to make the tent, to cover himself in the daytime instead of taking off his clothes.

He understood the strange reason why the Bedouins cross the desert at night, to protect themselves from the burning sands...

They are guided by the stars, clear skies without clouds, hidden paths in the firmament, invisible maps that lead to any place.

One must know how to look, the inexperienced in the desert does not look at the stars, but at the sands.

But, footprints in the sands fade as quickly as mirages.

He read a book that few read, he discovered another language, the language of silence, to hear the whispers of the wind, to let himself be ruled by the twinkling of the stars.

On his camel, he watched the changing color of the sand, the wind drew in the dunes paths. Dunes that appear and disappear, sudden storms do not allow the landscape to remain for long.

The old wanderer, a great master connoisseur of secrets, taught him how to navigate in the universe of the dunes.

He showed him another path, that of the soul, peace over adversity, patience in the face of eagerness, deep meditation after a mistake.

There is in the spirit the power to fail, no one escapes that power; when he wants to succeed.

Failure is learning, something difficult to understand, the struggle is abandoned when the test is demanding.

One gives up in the desperation that produces a mistake, ignoring that the required knowledge flows in the failed attempts.

Each time, one learns a little more, the success so longed for, does not consist in obtaining triumph and achievements.

Success is the wisdom to learn from small failures, in itself, success is the eternal chain formed from the links of mistakes.

Undoubtedly you will know more, the more you make mistakes.

Time marched on, each day assimilating the old man's secrets... one afternoon... arriving at the oasis, the desert dweller was in agony....

Kadaisha paused as he contemplated the emptiness of the precipice, the clouds dissipated. It gave a space for the monks to reflect, a camel driver, a life, the same life, that many had before entering the monastery.

The death of the desert dweller, shook the sands, he contemplated the agony, a body that is exhausted, but the essence was planted to be reborn.

The most valuable possession is knowledge, a seed not to be wasted, it is cultivated in work and action.

It is sown in the fertile soil of those who are willing to discover the deep knowledge of experience.

He prepared the stretcher with reeds, placed the corpse, tied it to an old camel also in agony, and left them to march.

It was his desert, he lived, he failed, he learned from it, and he will return to it, he looked at the path left by the trunks, time did not take long to erase it.

In a bonfire, he burned the few belongings, although one died, another desert dweller was born at the same time.

The days and nights passed in the infinite game of the hours, he knew the desert, the stars, the dunes, he knew how to read the small winds that warn where there is water, where the oasis are.

He knew the art of hunting, protecting himself and living in the sands.

He remembered the words of the dweller «The success in your life will be completed, when you teach how to avoid your failures.»

This is how the camel driver school was born, it still exists, there is no dweller, now they are like the stars that stud the sands.

The dweller did not look for apprentices, they came when, like him, they lost hope, failed in their first attempt, cried with fear in the dark.

One by one, they multiplied, in spite of that, they remembered the strength of the master who had no master, the great one, the one who learned from his failures.

It is not a legend, it happened in the beginning of time, the power to continue; it comes from the inner strength, when the need to survive strengthens the will.

Failure, when trying to light the fire, ends; when you learn to feel where the wind blows from.

And, for that, you will have to discover it, in the second, in the third or after many times.

Sometimes it happens that the longed-for success comes after the next simple failure.

You will never have a bonfire, you must fight to create a spark, sparks have no size, no matter how small they are, they produce fires.

Even the longed-for success, fortune, love, even time in its eternity, are born, from a penny, a failure, a glance and an instant.

If you can link one penny to another, you will have fortune, if you can link the instants, you will be the master of time.

It is not the story of a camel driver, it is the story hidden in the souls.

Throughout your life, in every step you take, in every illusion you forge in thought.

In the love you profess, in the wealth so longed for, in the triumph, there is hidden a terrible desert, ignorance.

There is no knowledge, no experience; before living through it.

Nobody lives anybody's life, it is the strange reason that impels to experiment, to try, to look for, to reach the triumph where another has failed.

Assuming it will be done, but, it will be but another failed attempt.

The ego's foolishness goes to extremes of anxiety, blind confidence in realizing what is not known.

That is good! Not to accept or defeat oneself, it is only a change of mental attitude.

To begin by accepting that the secrets are ignored, to launch oneself into the adventure of failure, to know that the more times one is shipwrecked, the greater the learning that one will have.

In doing so, the soul is strengthened, the will becomes iron, the feelings are harmonized, the challenge of a new adventure does not turn into resignation or failure.

What good is it for the beautiful seagull to have wings and wind, if it does not have the inner strength... to fly.

The snow that falls on the mountain is never the same, the icy wind does not come from the north, it changes with the moon and the stars.

Each person in his or her inner world should evaluate, what takes away harmony, what disturbs his or her senses, what has been the reason for failure.

Now, it is understood that, instead of seeking triumph and success, you should seek to fail in order to learn how to find it.

But, no! Seek to find failure as surrender, nor failure; as misfortune. Seek failure as wisdom, transform it into learning, discover the hidden knowledge that comes in adversity.

If you meditate on this, you will understand that you only learn by failing, you will be terrified to understand that success is nothing more than piling up failures. Now... you must meditate, if in your life you have failed or out of fear, you stopped learning, giving up on success.

The night vanished, Kadaisha vanished in the darkness where the torches had languished.

The monks, still, meditated, the failure so feared; now, it would be the most desired. To fail without collapsing is the mystery that success hides, but in itself, success as such does not exist, in the continuous learning of life and times, there is no end.

The monk wanted to return at that hour to the bridge of the stakes, he knew that he should fail to learn to feel, to see without seeing, to go ahead and fail, in order to pass it.

✱ Day Eight, Ninth, and Tenth
The arcane of seeing the invisible
Jian

Another day dawned, another lesson, he walked looking at the eight planks, at the end the monks were waiting, but he did not think about achieving it... now, he thought... about preparing himself.

Learning, that is the key, while learning, mistakes will appear, they are not a failure, he had to change the concept.

Kadaisha, appeared suddenly, you did not see him coming, as if he materialized, he was there.

- You guess that today you must learn another lesson, the one that will allow you to discover the strength of your inner self.

- Master, I have been meditating these days, I have understood that in the end, it is one who looks at life in different ways, without knowing how to act, no one ever taught me or at least hinted at the control one must have.

»To discover the path by oneself, without this "dweller of life", as I baptized it, is to live an empty life trying to get it right, pursuing success with eagerness, desire, passion, and only achieving failure.

- That's right, you are on the right path, you should reflect if at the end of these twenty-one days, you choose to be him, "the dweller of life".

»Outside the temple, few know the art of discerning, testing, exchanging the failure so ingrained for the learning necessary to build.

»The master builder who builds a house over the cliff, he did not succeed on the first attempt, he learned from others, many works collapsed before he succeeded, he, perceived that he was learning, so he never failed.

»Meditate on this, what must the master have first seen in his mind when he felt the impulse to undertake such a task?

- I guess the first thing was to deny the possibility, building on the edge of a cliff is not an easy thing to do, it is costly, it has risks, not only in building, but also that it will be destroyed if it goes wrong.

- Your mind leads you to the habitual, you see the problems, the denial, doubt, impossibility, are the barriers that lead to failure.

»For the great craftsman, it is a new challenge, where neither success nor failure exist.

»Before the opportunity, the first thing he does is to observe inside himself, if he has the knowledge and experience to do it and that, he has obtained it through building and destroying, learning the secrets.

»When he has meditated on his knowledge, he does the most important thing, he moves away from the mountain, for three days he will do nothing but contemplate.

»He will talk to the wind, he will listen to the whisper of the hillside, he will do what no one imagines, he will see the invisible of the abyss, that empty space that few will know, the greatest and most dangerous terror, the emptiness of the precipice.

»He will not master it, he will not be able to, on the contrary; he will merge with it for three days, he will feel how the winds ascend and descend, he will know the effect of the sun and the seasons.

»He will even contemplate the palpitation of the mountain when it expands or contracts with the full moon.

»No doubt he will dialogue and argue with the rain and the monsoon, more, he will do the prodigy, not by dominating or subduing them.

»He will merge with them, he will be the mountain, the wind, the rain, the abyss, he will feel the gentle sway of the moon, he will learn the rhythm of the seasons, so he will know how they will affect his work.

»With contemplation, he will understand how to do it, where the sleepers will go, the spaces for them to shrink in the winter and expand in the summer.

»You will know how the hours of sun and darkness make the mountain sleep and wake up, you will scrutinize its intimate arcana, it will be the so feared precipice, it will be the wind, the rain, in the end; it, it is the house.

»You will be the bridge, first in your mind, then your body will move in the Tai Chi of change, if you succeed You will be the bridge!

»Serás el puente, primero en tu mente, luego tu cuerpo se moverá en el Tai Chi del cambio, si lo logras ¡Tú serás el puente!

»Before you start meditating, get ready, get your food ready, your coat for the cold, see what you need for the journey within you, for three days.

»As you learn to be the bridge, your meditation will allow you to know yourself a little more, you will also be the elements, Fire, Water, Earth, Metal and Wood

»»From now on and for the rest of your existence, before doing any work, discover the Chi that is present, it is important that you do not ignore it, the elements change the course, discover its essence.

»It is hidden, within you and outside of you, if you do not harmonize your interior with your exterior, if you do not become the «One» you are going to fail until you understand it or without knowing it, you give up thinking that you have failed.

»You will not be able to see him with your physical eyes, nor feel him with your skin, although you are Chi, you must join it, to be it.

»Avoid fighting against the three days, forget the time, just imagine, feel, go inside yourself, what is outside doesn›t matter, in your mind three days can be a minute or a thousand years.

»Think, the time to get up will come, avoid anxiety, calm your spirit, concentrate on feeling.

I will teach you to see inside you, the bridge of Chi.

»Close your eyes, relax... breathe calmly... let your body feel light... let go of any tension you have, feel your legs, arms, hands, feel your face... enter into a state of harmony, breathe....

»Now; pass your hand in front of your closed eyes, you will see the difference between clarity and darkness, repeat it until you are aware that you perceive it.

»Concentrate on the clarity, it is similar to a deep sky, relaxing, do not lose your vision with the images that will appear.

»Leave your mind calm, control your thoughts, clarity, look at it... look for the farthest horizon....

»Keep looking, until you see discrete, distant, blurred colors appear, it is the first encounter with your Chi, keep looking....

»Different shades will appear, concentrate on one until all the clarity is of that color, the one you choose, it doesn't matter.

»Then... pick another color, keep going... it will be subtle, without force, the more relaxed your mind is, the more the color will flow from you.....

»When you manage to master the colors, you will look for the purple color, you will flood the whole vision, you are going to observe the farthest point...

»Behold it, concentrate... look at the background, suddenly you will see a spiral, rings coming towards you or coming out of you, let them flow.

»It is your inner energy... with your desire and will, you are going to make them come or go, fast or slow, one at a time or as many as you want, learn to manage them, it is your mind and your Chi.

»When you master them, something that will take you a little time, you are going to handle your energy, when the hoops come to you, your energy is the one that is flowing.

»When the hoops come out of you, you are receiving the outer chi. You must keep this in mind; when you go out of your state of visual meditation, leave your mental rings still, do not let them come or go, balance and harmony, make this a daily routine, each time you will achieve more progress, you will see great results in your life.

»Estás listo para meditar en los elementos que forman lo que quieres conocer, mira en tu mente, el Agua, el Fuego, la Tierra, el Metal y la Madera, que están en el puente, envueltos, en el Chi.

»Préstale la mayor atención a lo que no ves, el aire, el vacío entre los tablones, el viento, percibe el palpitar del corazón de los monjes, adelántate, siente la soga, únete a ella, sé la soga.

»Imagina todas las posibilidades, siente las suaves vibraciones, ve despacio, controla la ansiedad, comienza por la quietud... cuando sientas que estás preparado... ¡Hazlo!

- Master, what if I don›t accomplish it?

- You will have failed before starting, it is the first thought before the work, you declare in your interior that, you will not do it.

»You will justify your inability, your doubt, you will give up without beginning, if you give up in one work, always; you will give up in all.

»There is nothing preventing you from doing it, you already know, if you want to give up, the exit from the temple is in the palm trees, is that what you really want?

- No master, I'll go for things and I'll do it.

The monk prepared himself, some food, water, lamp with oil, fur robes for the coat, he put on his boots, gloves, and checked the five elements.

He started to contemplate the place, looking for where to meditate, he wanted to apply what Kadaisha suggested, which place is the best place to meditate for three days.

Where the wind comes from, where the snow falls more or less, where he will be able to sleep, he remembered the story of the camel driver, a thought in his mind surprised him «the dogs».

They know, he started with the options, for a while he investigated the behavior of the dogs living in the temple, they didn't sleep in the snow but in a corner, under a ledge.

«Dog food» another thought rumbled in his mind, he would need to sleep next to them.

He got the food, kept watching, concentrated on assessing the hazards of that spot, the roof, the accumulated snow, the emptiness that existed there and what it could be filled with.

Water, Fire, Metal, Wood and Earth, at that moment he understood the power of observing, mixing the five elements.

If the camel driver and he would have known about it, before embarking on any adventure, trip, business, romance, study, whatever, the five elements of Chi speak, no one knows how much the emptiness hides.

Thinking about it, he went back for another blanket, more water, food, oil, he preferred to have some left over, with this, he started a three day trip to the interior, at least that was what he supposed.

Near the kennel he settled in, tidied things up, just as the desert dweller did, order and priority, put on his coat and there he began to meditate.

On the top of a balcony, Kadaisha also contemplated him.

During the first hours he was restless, he could not concentrate, he fed the dogs, changed position, took off and put on his coat.

The normal process of harmonizing the mind, body and environment.

Small changes, the balance of the mind seeks equilibrium, accommodates itself by balancing the inside and the outside.

For three or four hours he meditated, at times throwing a few crumbs to the dogs, without leaving that stillness.

The shadows came with the snow, the dogs surrounded him, lying down, he fell asleep.

The dawn of the second day he sat in deep meditation, it is not known at what time he began.

The afternoon... there was no movement, only an image of deep serenity, Kadaisha had not moved from the balcony either.

Master and pupil, united by emptiness.

The gloom covered the temple, the snow ceased, the candle gave no light, the monk found the path to his inner self.

Third day, hours of stillness, the food, the coat, were intact, even the dogs' food was there.

Kadaisha approached without interrupting, carefully led the dogs away, leaving the monk in solitary surroundings.

Fourth day, the same, nothing changes, in the temple, from time to time the monks manage to enter so deep in their minds, that they lose themselves from reality, it is a deep state of contemplation.

In a kind of reverie, one begins to see the Chi, the rings, the mind goes inside them, the interior is in harmony.

Almost at dusk, the monk returned, he came out of that state, hungry and thirsty, he got up looking for the dogs, they were not there.

Somewhat disoriented, other monks watched him from afar. He picked up his things and went to the temple, where Kadaisha was.

- Master, I don't think I succeeded, it was only a short time that my body endured. I am sorry if I have failed you.

- You can never fail anyone, if so, you fail yourself. You don't know how much time has passed?

-No Master, maybe one day, I don't know, I saw the rings in my mind, at first it was difficult, then, they appeared, I started to play by changing their color.

»And then, in a moment, in the background a light appeared, far away and small, I felt that it attracted me.

»I felt I was going towards the light, a while later, it was something celestial... refulgent colors, fantastic rainbows, I don›t know how to describe them.

»I could feel the light, it was the light, I was ecstatic, I did not want to get out of there, Master, I did not imagine that something like that existed, there are no words to describe, it is to feel poetry.

»Being there, I thought about the bridge, I saw that it was alive, I saw the trees from where the timbers were taken, the origin of the ropes, the soul of the monks, the wind, I knew the secrets, Master, I think I spoke with the essence of life

- Five days have passed since you started. You have discovered your Chi, your inner power, you opened the door of the living force, from now on use your gift wisely.

- Five days, Master, really?

»Master, something strange happened while I was there, I could see myself, it is strange, I saw myself incandescent, surrounded by a strong light.

- Come, drink tea, listen carefully to what you should know.

»The monks do not succeed in the first attempt to enter the Chi, with dedication they discover it, you did it!

»Within each being dwells trapped the power, the force that governs life, destinies, existence, it is the primary energy of creation.

»The majority, waste time searching outside of itself, in the world or in the underworld, in the light or in the infinite night.

»In gold or in beauty, they seek it in others, always, outside of themselves.

»They ignore that the force that governs all forces is there, inside their skin, deep in their thoughts, so close that they do not see it.

»However; they perceive it, they intuit that it exists, at times, the power flows; managing to achieve what in their vision they consider a success.

»Others block it by thoughts, denial, limitations, some imposed by harmful influences, loneliness, absence of struggle, fears, bad company, close the door to the flow of power, destroyed loves that destroy souls.

»When you discover it, you possess the gift of power, having it, it must be accompanied by great responsibility. As it builds, it also destroys.

»Be careful when you do this, the rings you saw in your contemplation indicate that, as you radiate it, so you also receive it, whatever you do with it, always keep it in mind! It will return to you.

»Greed, power, domination, riches, uncontrolled sexuality, passing luxuries, the desire to possess the material, break the balance of the five elements, the Chi comes into conflict, chaos will come in the incessant rhythm of existence, nothing lasts.

»In the measure of time, darkness, abandonment, destruction, scarcity, poverty, lovelessness, is a trapped Chi.

»In any of the extremes, will, desire, contemplation and meditation, help return to harmony. If this is achieved, power is conquered.

»To harmonize your spirit, your mind must let go, empty the cup that is already full and blinds your reason, leading you to the terrible darkness of suffering.

»The memories, the experiences, the acceptance of the supposed defeat, the disdain to live must be transmuted, if you do not do it, harmony will not be in your life.

»No matter how hard you try, nothing will go right, you will desire change in an instant, understand; the further you move away from your center, so will be the path of return.

»Under the art of discipline, exigency, constancy you will manage to walk the path of return, be careful of the other extreme.

»The universe will not change for you, no one will, it is you who cleans your interior and initiates the change. It is you, the change!

»As you empty the cup of your life, you start another, it is where you will have to learn to use your power. You live by it or for it. A difficult decision.

»You must learn, you will make mistakes to do so, mastering strength requires discovering it. That will happen when you fail, so you will know what or not to do.

»Master your mind and your inner power, then you will master controlling the world.

»Now you must train, apply what you have learned until you cross the bridge, you choose.

✻ Day Eleven
Jundong
The arcane of movement

The monk listened attentively, undoubtedly something marvelous had happened inside him.

The door opened to this other world, as he quieted his mind and body, the spirit flowed in its maximum splendor.

A new beginning, the chaos with which he arrived at the temple had disappeared, the serene mind, clear, now showed him another horizon.

He stared at the bridge of twenty-one steps over the moat of stakes. In the distance, the bridge over the ropes, the monks were still waiting for him, he could not escape this encounter.

He sat down to contemplate the two bridges and the moat, a garden of stakes in the background, different sizes, he said to himself "Why not walk on the stakes?" a daring decision.

However, he preferred to conclude with the lesson, he had to practice, train and use his new senses for the first time.

He perched on the eight-step bridge, he could not see the eyes of the monks, they were covered by the hood. Standing on the first step, he contemplated the wind, Earth, Fire, Wood, Metal and Water, he related each element to something on the bridge, before trying anything, he took off his shoes, now he could see with other senses.

The feet on the plank transferred all the vibrations, he even managed to perceive, after hours of being there, the beating of the monks' hearts.

It was not his eyes or ears, he was merging with the bridge. For that day he did nothing else.

Lying in the snow, looking at the sky, he meditated on what had happened, each part of the days that had passed, his hands on the snow allowed him to perceive other sensations, the unknown of a new energy, which, although it is always there, few feel it.

He closed his eyes, voluntarily flooded his vision looking for color, his breath was fading, he wanted to be in that place of light, to feel the power, the vital force of Chi.

He lost himself inside his being, in the deep abyss that leads to the union with the Whole.

The hours passed, the night and the snow covered the temple, near dawn, there was a bustle, something that does not usually happenr.

The monks ran to the ledges of the balconies, while they murmured, asking questions;

- *Did he find it? Did he find it?*

- *Yes, answered others, look around. Look at it!*

Down below, in deep meditation, a circle of snow could be seen around him, as if a bell was protecting him, somehow, power was sensed.

- *¡He found enlightenment! Someone shouted.*

- In such a short time, he must be an initiate who did not know?

The monks were all talking, the light some had found and others were searching, eagerly, for enlightenment. Kadaisha looked out onto the balcony, all were silent, waiting to hear him.

- A new master has been born, the paths of wisdom lead the apprentice to discover the master that dwells within. Just like you, they discover it in a different way.

One of the nuns, who had entered the temple some time before, said to him:

- Master, what makes some find enlightenment like him and others not?

- The paths to wisdom are varied and different, the experiences of each one bring them closer or further away from their essence, the experiences that seem destructive lead you to reflect, it is the first step to enter within you

Enlightenment is in each one of us, at the same time you are a beginner, a student, an apprentice and a master. It depends on which one you want to stay in or if you want to move forward.

»You have the power; it is your mind, the fear, the fear of losing the memories and attachments that create the barrier between enlightenment and the meaning of life.

»A life of apparent suffering, defeats and failures, detaches the mind from the material world, loneliness, contempt, agony, exhausting the desire to live.

»It is that moment where you evaluate existence, a dangerous instant that either leads to death or to life.

»If you find the right path, you free yourself from mental ties, there is nothing material that binds your spirit, in doing so you discover it.

»It is when you clean the inner vessel, you enter into harmony and there, you discover enlightenment.

»Outside the temple, thousands, millions of masters who rose from adversity, those who lost, those who suffered sorrow, illness, betrayal, pain, death, those who were once despised, found the light within.

»I do not mean that one must suffer to find it, others discover the light by contemplating and valuing life.

»It is not something you can learn, it is something you let flow from within you, when you go inside and open the door.

»The key to wisdom is simple to find, at the same time it is difficult to apply, few achieve it, when you lose the balance between your inner self and your world, you move away from the essence.

»The value of life is not in possessing, nor in showing off or achieving fame and fortune, the value is in cultivating the seed that you bring to this world when you incarnate.

»Thus, as nature does, you will be the fruit and the seed for other lives. Many live equal incarnations, until in one they find enlightenment and advance. If not, what would be the profound meaning of existence?

»To find enlightenment; is to understand that this universe is temporary, ephemeral, that, although it is presumed that one has it, in the background the inner essence endures.

»Cuando comprendas... que eres un huésped de tu cuerpo y descubras el huésped que lo habita, comenzarás a descubrir el poder.

Otherwise, you live in a body, in a physical world far from your being, know the elements, the more Earth you are, the less Chi you will have.

»Bring your mind, body and spirit into balance, you will undoubtedly find your enlightenment, you are already on the path, continue without eagerness, you will know when you arrive.

»Keep in mind, you inhabit a material body in a physical world, your essence is not.

- *Master, who dwells in my body?*

- *You!*

The monk sat up, his countenance was different, there was no longer the joy of the first time.

More controlled and serene, he arranged the hood, went to the dining room looking for food, the body requires it no matter how much power there is.

To let go, it is not about annulling, it is to maintain harmony without repressing oneself, the body has needs, in fact, in the temple there is a place where tantric sexuality is taught, the handling of sex; outside of emotions, where another energy flows.

He took some time talking with other monks, he told his experience, he showed the path, his path, each one must discover his own.

The experiences of life transport the soul to confines or prisons.

The monks; they had lived different experiences that led them to the temple, at the beginning, seeking refuge.

✳ Days Twelve and Thirteen
Zhang Arcanum
The wall

Time passes in the temple in a different way with the world around it, there are no clocks or calendars, they are governed by the moon and the seasons.

The days follow one another, the hours are different for each monk, some train during the day, others prefer the shadows of darkness.

The power in all things is also discovered, few have seen the power of those who dominate the Fire. Apprentices and masters, who at the same time are apprentices.

Just like the Water Master, melted forever in the well. He ventured with the planks, he began to feel more than with his skin, with his energy, he contemplated, not the beam, but the eight steps.

The monks moved the ropes, he was ahead of the movement keeping his balance. There was no eagerness, serene he went with the rhythm, he took advantage of the movement to advance.

When the monk let go and the wood returned, he advanced, when the wood moved away, he remained still, balancing.

The movement that primates perform in the jungle with the branches, when they approach, they take them and let themselves go, when they move away, they do not look for them. It is knowing how to wait for the right moment.

For two days, he walked the eight steps many times, and at the end, blindfolded, he crossed them again and again.

No matter the movement, he was the bridge.

Kadaisha approached.

- *Now what do you think?*

- *Master, in spite of having these new sensations, I am haunted by the fear of doing it on the other bridge. I have doubts of making it, the stakes of the moat I see them in my dreams going through my body.*

- It is the Zhang, something you must overcome, it is the wall, the barrier, that your mind creates to stop your power.

»They are your fears, ghosts that emerge in the night of your thought. Memories that linger..

»To feel fear is normal, you should not overcome it, know it! Make it your ally, melt with your fear.

»Overcoming your wall is not an easy task, you will have to confront your deepest and most ingrained fears, you will have to empower your existence.

»The agitated sea of your soul, you will have to calm it, you will fall many times, you will want to give up, you will feel that it is not worth fighting, the wall will always want to triumph over you.

»You should use your wisdom, know your wall, what is it made of?

»Chi or wind, they are the walls caused by the mind, your past, accumulated fears, illusions, desire.

»The suffering of love is one of the most difficult to demolish, only freedom does it.

»Exhausted illusions, wasted opportunities, death, loneliness, that wall, nullifies your existence.

»Wood Zang, is that of your body and possessions, lost riches, disease, destruction, poverty.

»In the wall of Water, you find family, parents, children, your nation, your culture, social dejection or triumph.

»You have the wall of Fire, anger, hatred, spite, violence, ignorance, contempt. Or the illusions of passion, ecstasy, frenzy, uncontrolled sexuality, daring.

»One that is difficult to break down, against which you must fight, is that of Metal:

«Gold that nothing eats away at it; it will eat away at your soul» Beware of that wall!

»One you can never break down, Heian of siwang, the wall of your physical death, Chi, has no walls. As long as your body allows you to live, you have the power to break them down.

»As soon as you undertake something, you will have to look at the ones that trap you, face them! You will have to fill yourself with decisions, to evaluate, to contemplate, to search within yourself for your limitations.

»Stay away from what you want to conquer, contemplate it, melt yourself, be one.

»You will feel it inside of you when you must move forward, go slowly, do not lose control, fear keeps you alert, it warns you, do not fight against it, turn it into your ally, the bridge awaits you.

Twenty-one planks over the stake pit, a challenge not only physical but mental.

The mind, will, discipline and constancy are the solid bases to achieve progress in any enterprise.

However, in the eagerness of the life one wishes to have the power, one dreams to obtain the force, the stories, legends of great heroes who possess incredible capacities.

To want to see with the mind, to travel in the spirit, in an unfolding, to perceive the future, to have inner strength, to be able to work mental wonders.

One wants to have success, luck, joy, love, happiness, to reach the summits of desires, to live fully.

One wants it to happen immediately, but few manage to at least begin an inner construction. Immediacy has become the purpose of achievement, wanting to obtain knowledge, training and wisdom in an instant. It starts with encouragement, it is demanded, soon decaying, giving up.

The power flows, gushes drop by drop, until it forms the sea.

Learning to dominate the mind is an art that requires time and dedication, a constant work, the deeper you go inside yourself, the greater the power that radiates outward.

It is the lamp that is lit, it possesses the inexhaustible fuel, illuminating the exterior, it radiates its maximum splendor without wishing to do so.

All existence, with its ups and downs and apparent failures, is mutable, the mind is in charge of creating universes of destruction, it impoverishes the soul, it prevents the force from freeing itself, the imagination; a dying prisoner in the prison created with thought.

One lives a constant struggle, denial vibrates perpetually inhibiting progress, one goes against the current instead of getting out of the turbulent channel of life.

A pause in daily life, a moment of contemplation, an instant to begin to walk the intimate path, where one finds the key that opens all the locks. It is not easy to access power, the time required to achieve it does not exist, it happens in a second or in a thousand lives.

There are many beings who have found the power of Chi in a terrible instant, a blow that annuls dignity, a humiliating insult, an accident, misfortune, the tragic and adverse, are keys that open the power.

When dignity is mistreated, the ego subjugated, subjected to the hell of contempt, the spirit awakens.

Some fight, take advantage of that moment to empower themselves, the pain opens the door abruptly, they shout: Enough! To stop accepting the begging of the soul.

It is there, when the power begins to flow, in an instant, even if the acceptance is constant and the justification is present, in a thousand lives, it will not be achieved.

The strength is felt above the sadness, unhappiness and adversity, it is a process that begins when it is perceived that there is nothing.

The maximum limitation is in thinking, that thought of yesterday prevents progress, if the cup is not emptied abandoning the past, the desired future will not come.

In crying, a product of the most intense pain, it strengthens the soul or submerges it in the deepest dungeons of suffering.

It is the mind that makes the difference, the self-love, the dignity, the strength to live.

✻ Day Fourteen, Fifteen and Sixteen The Arcane of Indecision Yourouguaduan

Another day, the moat of stakes seemed to glow, the apprentice, contemplating the floating bridge, gazed at the height, if he were to fall, his body would be pierced and die.

The monks were not there, when a monk prepared to test himself, the others moved away, it is a solitary process, without spectators.

It is overcoming one's own wall, an inner decision, a conflict with oneself. Kadaisha, wrapped in his robe, was the only companion.

- It is not easy to take a step for change, in your mind now a battle rages, between your will, your desire and your fear.

»It is the pit where the stone has fallen and lifts the silt, you do not see the bottom. Allow it to decant, don't look at the stake pit, don't look at the bridge as something you have to overcome.

»Look at it as something that lifts you up, just like the crane when it is ready to fly, don't look at the abyss, look at the freedom of the infinite sky, when it is time to fly, it will fly.

- Master, it is difficult to take the step, the thoughts If I fall and die? How great is the agony of my body being pierced?

- Is that what you think? For a moment, look inside yourself, What do you perceive? Your fears of dying, but don't you discover, the strength of living as you pass the bridge.

»Indecision is a Jin Gui, the ghostly being that appears in front of your uncertain future, it nests in your mind showing you adversity and misfortune, it makes you evaluate the risks, it is a sage hidden in the penumbra of your soul.

»It slows you down and limits you, it is the mountain that clouds itself so that you do not see it, it is your projected fears that destroy your courage.

»If you are not sure of your readiness, don't do it, wait for the moment, even the birds at the edge of the cliff do not venture to challenge the wind.

»Indecision is wisdom, when you meditate on the consequences, the Jin shows you your fears, if you do not overcome them, they will destroy you.

»When this happens, you consider that you are not ready, you have no security, take the time you require to inquire within yourself, practice, know, prove yourself, until within yourself; you are one with what you desire.

»Failures in life occur when you throw yourself in pursuit of a desire, when without knowing, your ego incites you to face the unknown.

»Come, let us go to the moat, you will contemplate the bridge from below, you will know the stakes, but do not touch the dead, do not interrupt the dreams of those who ventured without being ready.

- Master, Is indecision bad?

- There is nothing bad or good, indecision warns you that it is not yet the time to act, listen to it, do not fight against it, contemplate the options you have, embark on your journey when you feel you must.

As he spoke, they descended into the moat, the perspective changes, the bridge is seen caressing the sky, the tips of the stakes disappear, the skeletons protruded from the snow, it was terrifying.

- Now that you have a different vision of your goal, something you should have done before, know the corners. The tiger before hunting merges with its territory, knows each labyrinth, learns from its mistakes.

»Contemplate the invisible, the wind swirling under the bridge will make you lose your balance. Today, contemplate what you were missing, look at the tip of the stakes.

»What you don›t see at the beginning, is the first thing you must see.

KKadaisha left and the apprentice remained contemplating another universe, he did not imagine that it was different, he began to walk through each part, he looked at the remains scattered thinking about the life of the dead monks, he could not intuit that he would talk to them.

He obeyed avoiding touching them, the shiver of death ran through him. Being there, he felt attracted to a special stake, he saw it vibrating, he perceived its strange energy, somehow, it was different from the others.

Lying down on the snow, he stuck his head against the wood looking at the tip towards the sky, he saw the clouds move, the wind pushed the snow over the pit, somehow, again he entered into a deep meditation.

Four days and nights passed before the monk returned from his vision. Kadaisha was the only one who knew he was there. From time to time he would visit the pit, allowing his apprentice to continue to discover his power.

✻ Day Seventeen, Eighteen, Nineteen and Twenty
The arcane of awakening
Zhoamíng

One strange day, Master Li Lian Cheng, was with the apprentice in the garden of stones, a place in the temple where some monks train walking on small pebbles.

Master Li, is Shifu, master of Kung fu, Tai Chi and martial arts, he has a great philosophy, there are many legends about him, some say he was the first enlightened of the temple.

No one knows his age and there is no way to intuit it, they say he dominates the Chi at will, he knocks down another man at a distance. He discovered another path to enlightenment by copying the movement of the wind, clouds and animals.

During training, teachings of how to walk on the stones, while executing the celestial movements of the Tai were taught.

It is flowing with the wind, beyond this, it is "Meditation in Movement" an art, where the mind is lost to the rhythm that the body dances.

It is not in the temple where it is performed, in daily life, in the office, at home, in the different jobs Tai is performed.

Take a breath, relaxing the mind and body, be aware of each movement allowing it to flow. Concentration is to be in the world, but isolated from the world.

One of the exercises when entering the temple is sweeping, a humble job that at the beginning is considered as contempt or slavery.

Master Li learned Tai by sweeping, he said that in doing so he read the life of those who left the debris, he moved the broom with the wind of thought, he knew the secrets of the monks, he discovered that sweeping allows the flow of Chi, both one's own and that of the place that is swept.

When the mind is in conflict, one should seek Tai movement, the stillness in the face of failure, difficulty, loneliness, depression, sadness or melancholy.

The states of alteration and tension increase, the Tai is the movement, it does not matter if you do not know the katas. Running, swimming, dancing, doing any sport, whatever involves movement is Tai, if accompanied with meditation, it becomes Tai-Chi. Meditate with movement.

The following days, the monk dedicated himself to walk on the stones, moving as the master indicated, so slow that he seemed not to move.

An inner learning, preparation.

It was the twenty-first day. In the temple, the days of the moon's growth start from the new moon, seven days before the full moon, any action that is executed with discipline, during the twenty-one lunar days or twenty-three solar days, becomes a habit.

Waking up during this time at the same hour, doing a specific repetitive activity, setting a task.

It is the time needed to adapt with the new, whether it be a job, a change, or a relationship. Twenty-one moon days, the time it takes for the seasons to change.

The apprentice, who came in despair at the apparent failure, was about to prove that; failure does not exist. Just as success does not exist either, both are a constant learning. The experience to discover the infinite world of alternatives and options.

⁎ Day Twenty-One
The arcane of the beginning
Kaishi

Nothing suggested any kind of ritual or anything different, the snow had stopped falling, the sky was clear and cloudless, a day like every other day.

Master Li and Kadaisha were close to the apprentice, on the other side of the bridge two monks were waiting, Master Li took him to the edge of the planks, Kadaisha was a spectator.

- Do you feel sure that this is what you wish to do today?

- No, master, but I will wait for the unexpected, I cannot be sure of something that I have not realized, I feel that it is the moment to do it, I will not postpone this event any longer, if I do not do it today, I will never do it.

- You have the power within. You have discovered a different awakening. It is the beginning of another horizon in your life or the beginning of another life, it will depend on you. Go and discover your power.

The teachers moved away, leaving him the space, the three monks, one at the beginning, two at the end of the bridge. The image stood out, the bridge, the stake pit, the monks, a deep stillness was reflected.

He took off his sandals, his bare feet landed on the steps before the first plank, which he would have to reach by stretching and raising his leg.

He would have to calculate the perfect momentum, so as not to overshoot or lose his balance and fall into the stake pit.

The activity with Master Li allowed him to do it like when a feline jumps, so fluid that he seemed to float.

He stood still on the first plank, for an hour, the monks pulling and releasing the ropes, making the bridge move. He felt and perceived the environment, with the different and imperceptible vibrations.

He began to move rhythmically to the impulse of the timbers, with the agility of those who travel from tree to tree, he crossed the bridge.

There were no congratulations, the monks released the ropes and left. He looked at the stake pit, looked at the bridge, which without the tension of the ropes was even more unstable, and crossed it again, standing in the center looking down.

Then, with all the serenity, without caring about the movements, he descended.

He encountered Kadaisha...

- You overcome your fears, you did you! Has it been a success in your life or a failure?

- Master; since the day I arrived dejected by a life of adversities, I was blind, I always thought I was doomed to misfortune, nothing in me to exist, I managed to conclude it.

»Thanks to your teachings I have discovered another world, not outside of me, but inside, deep inside, there is no failure if you venture to continue overcoming it.

» I understood in the same way that the longed-for success is nothing more than a passing apprenticeship.

»The steps of the bridge are just steps that depending on the training become advancement or decay. The first day I assumed that bridge could never be crossed. Today, it is different, my mind has been cleansed of the limitations, I have overcome my walls, crossing it is not success, it is one more step.

- You have achieved the awakening, it is you who entered inside you, to that sacred and intimate place of your being, no one will accompany you.

»Failure and success are two states of the soul, for the yellow turtle inside the comfort of the egg is his life, the day comes when he must leave it, he must fight to get out of the deep nest, face the adversity of predators, while he reaches the sea.

»With all the strength; strength born of her innate power the turtle survives, the adversity is not considered as failure, nor achievement as success.

»The turtle does not victimize or fills itself with self-pity, it does not destroy the inner self by giving up, it never gives up, it knows one must prepare for the worst storms or the calm days, deep down in the essence it knows it has the power.

»In the temple there are no graduations, you carry that in your spirit. I hope you have found some answers to what you came to seek, now you are free to follow your path.

- *Master, no, so far I have begun. Should I leave the temple?*

- *Not if you don't want to. If you do stay, what do you want to do?*

- *Master, I want to cross the moat, walk on the points of the stakes. The bridge is a step, the path is the moat.*

- You overcome your fears, you did you! Has it been a success in your life or a failure?

- Master; since the day I arrived dejected by a life of adversities, I was blind, I always thought I was doomed to misfortune, nothing in me to exist, I managed to conclude it.

»Thanks to your teachings I have discovered another world, not outside of me, but inside, deep inside, there is no failure if you venture to continue overcoming it.

» I understood in the same way that the longed-for success is nothing more than a passing apprenticeship.

»The steps of the bridge are just steps that depending on the training become advancement or decay. The first day I assumed that bridge could never be crossed.

Today, it is different, my mind has been cleansed of the limitations, I have overcome my walls, crossing it is not success, it is one more step.

- You have achieved the awakening, it is you who entered inside you, to that sacred and intimate place of your being, no one will accompany you.

»Failure and success are two states of the soul, for the yellow turtle inside the comfort of the egg is his life, the day comes when he must leave it, he must fight to get out of the deep nest, face the adversity of predators, while he reaches the sea.

»With all the strength; strength born of her innate power the turtle survives, the adversity is not considered as failure, nor achievement as success.

»The turtle does not victimize or fills itself with self-pity, it does not destroy the inner self by giving up, it never gives up, it knows one must prepare for the worst storms or the calm days, deep down in the essence it knows it has the power.

»In the temple there are no graduations, you carry that in your spirit. I hope you have found some answers to what you came to seek, now you are free to follow your path.

- Master, no, so far I have begun. Should I leave the temple?

- Not if you don't want to. If you do stay, what do you want to do?

- Master, I want to cross the moat, walk on the points of the stakes. The bridge is a step, the path is the moat.

To be continued…

Note from the author

The stories of Kadaisha the monk are a series of reflections on the themes of the soul, each one brings knowledge and meditation. They are sequences without order of the different situations that sometimes disturbs life.

When the path is lost and reason is clouded, these meditations allow you to discover your inner strength. Each story is a part of Kadaisha's magic book.

THE MASTER OF THE STAKES

Encyclopedia Universe of Magic

Want to learn magic?

Enter the school of magic through our encyclopedia in Ofiuco Wicca. The hidden power of the mind, the influence without space or time. A knowledge kept for millennia, now in your hands.

www.editorialwicca.com

www.ingramcontent.com/pod-product-compliance
Lightning Source LLC
LaVergne TN
LVHW041111150826
845673LV00007B/2008

* 9 7 9 8 3 6 8 1 6 0 8 5 6 *